WILLIAM SA

HOW MEN

TEST

WOMEN

8 PSYCHOLOGICAL WAYS MEN TEST THE WOMEN THEY LIKE

Table of Contents

INTRODUCTION

With the essential people in their lives, men continue to struggle with understanding and expressing their feelings, inner anxieties, and insecurities, which has an influence on intimacy and their capacity to grow and connect with women. When it comes to dating and long-term relationships, too many women repeatedly go against themselves in a variety of ways. This causes a lot of the drama, pain, and confusion that women go through in their romantic lives that they wouldn't have to go through if they were more strong and trusted of themselves

Smart men test women. If a man doesn't test a woman, it may be a sign of disinterest in emotional relationships or he is inexperienced in relationships. Men will test you to better understand your character or to test you to know how compatible you are with him. Often women are so willing to do anything to be with a man.

We can be stupid because we are emotional creatures.

Men know it.

They use our vulnerabilities to their advantage until they understand what they want from us. Sometimes a man takes our devotion further than what is said, because he knows that many women devote all their energy to love. And that we give up our pride and confidence all too easily. You may think that we present ourselves more on the surface. So men test women to discover their depths, strengths, and limits and to see what they can and cannot do.

In the early stages of a relationship, you go through the part where you both feel for each other, connect and learn from each other to see how you fit together with serious potential. And he has a strategy. He plays mind games and tricks.

Now, how you handle this test will set the tone for your relationship or your lack of relationship.

Three Reasons Why Men Can Test Women

1. Baggage Test

Suppose you want to know first whether you are short-term or long-term material. He then needs to know which line you're pulling, how heavy it is, and whether you really deserve the effort it takes to share the load before he intervenes.

TIP

And that there is a key for every woman dealing with a man testing the load on the cock. You don't have to "fix" yourself before starting a new relationship, but getting to know yourself will keep you on track to getting what you need and want in your partner. It will also save you from getting caught in something toxic. It has to be amazing. You have to feel right. Like "wise men" testing women, we too must be selective about who deserves our time and heart before we love too much and fall too low. And ideally, before we find ourselves in the confusing emotional torment caused by a man using strategic testing to uncover our status value or worse, keeping us hanging with no intention of taking advantage of love. Nothing emerges in a relationship without baggage. We all have queues. Mature women need a mature and responsible partner who can fully embrace their burdens (and vice versa) or just leave the image.

She didn't need a man to flip her coin.

She needs a man who is on the same page as her.

2. Tug-o-war

Are you sweet, caring, and kind?
This is a terrific attribute, but if you're too eager to do what they want, some guys will take you for granted. They'll start to think of you as a mother, sister, or doormat, and you don't want to be in that situation. Men who put women to the test are usually seeking for

strong, self-assured women who know what they want. He's trying to see how many bent balls he can hurl at you and how many you can keep. He was looking for the unexpected. He admires a feisty woman who is faithful to her views and fights fiercely for what she wants.

He'll pull a woman's strings and put her strength to the test in order to evaluate how she manages obstacles and situations, as well as how confident she is in dealing with them.

TIP

Yes, guys enjoy the thrill of pursuing a woman who understands what she wants out of life, but if you suspect she's playing games with you, call her.

He undoubtedly wanted to know that not everything was in his hands.

When he tries to make you feel awful or direct it towards you, he's still playing mind games. And, to be honest, that's not a quality you'd want in someone who truly cares about you.

Men who aren't honest with themselves about what they want or don't want are their own (and your) worst enemies. I'm not sure about you, but I'd rather know where I stand with a guy than spend our time with nonsense about power struggles.

When a man is serious and capable of handling the warmth of a woman's love and emotions, on the other hand, his desire for a powerful woman deepens. Among all the swinging clubs, men are the most sensitive creatures.

He undoubtedly wanted to know that not everything was in his hands.

And a woman should be certain that she can present herself to him with the attributes that are appropriate for her love. He needs to know that he is capable of making his own life decisions and that he will not reject him because of fan-related nonsense.

In relationships, it creates a sense of equality.

3. He tests you to know how much you value and respect yourself

How much do you value your own self-respect? How much value do you place on yourself? Are you going to put some limits in place?

Will you confront him if he continues to be a jerk?

The silent treatment. The feeling of remorse. The ruse of gaslighting. The yo-yo games are a lot of fun. It's the poker game you didn't ask to play. The one where a man has placed you at a table without your knowledge, putting you to the test to see what he can get away with and if you can set clear boundaries. You will set the boundaries if you value yourself. He learns to trust and respect you when you set the boundaries. And don't be deceived by his beautiful grin and intriguing brains; he knows what is and isn't suitable. He's fully aware of the lines he crosses and the cheap tricks he has up his sleeve, and he's interested in seeing which poker love-hand you're ready to accept.

"How much longer will she have to wait for me?"

"Will she do my laundry?" I inquire.

"Will you cook for me?"

"Why do you keep coming back when I treat her badly?"

"Are you going to ignore her?"

TIP

Yeah. No. You aren't the Joker. You're a Queen with an Ace of Self-Love. Keep that in mind while he seeks ego play at the round table. Men require the feeling of being desired and appreciated. Women, too, share this trait. The difference is that men frequently attain their purpose by manipulating women. It also makes them feel powerful.

If a woman relies on a guy for reassurance and makes all of her decisions, or if he learns that she will never speak up for fear of upsetting the status quo. He won't trust her after that because he can get away with whatever he wants. This is something you don't want to happen. It entails a loss of dignity. Because getting a clingy and needy woman is way too simple, sensible guys (the ones you want) go after women who exude confidence. Chasing a powerful woman is perfectly up their alley, so they go for it.

That means you have to remember that you are a queen — treat yourself like one — be confident in your feminine and assured with who you are in the in-between space when he tests your worth.

How Men Test Women

1. The Casual Relationship Test

In this century, many single men who previously had multiple women would try to see if they could maintain a casual relationship in the early stages of a relationship.

A casual relationship is a type of relationship that allows a person to benefit from the relationship without actually being official in that relationship.

To pass this test, don't give a man any advantage in a casual relationship. This benefit goes beyond sexual intimacy, it means being there for him every step of the way, but he doesn't do the same for you.

2. The Jealousy Test

This happens when a guy intentionally tries to make you jealous by flirting with your friends or other women around you to see how you will react. This is very different from a guy who wants to cheat on you, because if he is interested in cheating on you or dating another woman, he will definitely not choose your friends or the people you hang out with, but will try to see how you will react to his behavior.

Will you be mad or mad at him? Would you defend your position and call him about his behavior? He's also trying to convince you that you love and care about him.

According to him, if you are jealous, you will definitely love him and care for him, but if you are indifferent, it shows that you really don't care about him.

How do you pass this test:
Understand that he is flirting because he wants you to be jealous and hopes that it

triggers an emotional respond from you, instead give him no reaction at all. What you should do is ignore his behavior and do not give him any emotional reaction, engage in a conversation with someone else, leave the area and go somewhere else. Just do whatever you can to ignore his behavior no matter how hard it is. If he feels it isn't working, he is going to feel like you really aren't that into him or that you don't care as much and when that happens he is going to work hard to gain your love and affection.

3. Are You A Loyal Woman Test

When a man starts to fall for a woman, he starts to have one important question that really bothers him this question is

"is she a loyal person?".

A guy will test you in various ways to see if he can trust you. In particular, he wants to know if you are a woman who is not easily seduced or flattered by other men who may be prettier or richer than her. He will begin to subtly test your feelings while the two of you are talking. He will bring up situations where someone cheats on their partner and asks for your opinion.

In this case, he is trying to gain access to your values in a hypothetical situation. Most guys can go a step further by asking their male friends to flirt with you to see how you react.

The question here is: are you flirting back? Do you set good boundaries with his friends? And most importantly, will you tell him about it?

If you are really into your man, you will not flirt with his friends. The real test here is if you can communicate back to him and let him know what happened and also calmly discussing what you experienced.

4. The Bro test

Here a guy who really likes a girl is going to take her out with his friends and see how she reacts. You don't have to like the things men do or do what they love or drink lots of beer to connect with them. All you have to do is simply ask the guys about themselves. Let them express themselves and connect with them by asking them what they do for fun, asking them where they like to go out at night, asking questions about the guy you're dating, that way you can connect with your friends.

The psychological trick is to get them to talk about themselves, this way you will easily pass the test.

5. Do You Have A Life Test

When two people are in relationship, the two people glue together and become one. During this dating or courting period, differences are bound to arise, problems and preferences will present themselves. It is during this time that a man will test you to see if he is your whole life or if you are able to maintain a healthy balance. In other words, he will test you to see if he can get you to change your mind about something that was very important to you before you met him.

For example; you had dinner plans with your girlfriend and made that plan a week in advance, yet he calls you to ask you to go out on a date with him. When you remind him that you had dinner plans with your girlfriend, he acts like he completely forgot about it or never knew about it, then he goes ahead to ask you if you can reschedule with her because he is bored.

This test is a problem on so many levels.

First, it is completely selfish and unacceptable for anyone to make that request of you by trying to make you choose him over your girlfriend despite the fact that you established plans with her .

If you respond by saying " I will check and reschedule with her, no big deal" Then you are letting him know he can break your life's habit and thereby putting you out of balance

Secondly, you'll come across as a pushover and he will begin to lose respect for you. That sends a message to him that he is your whole life, that you are clingy and no high value man would want that.

To handle this: make him know that you are a person that values relationships and a person that keeps her word. Therefore, maintain the friendship and habits that you had before you met him and also invite him into your life. This balance and it is healthy.

6. Do You Value And Respect Yourself Test

This test is part of the reason a man tests a woman. Most men do not intentionally plan to test your self-respect. It happens in situations where you both have disagreements or conflicts. It happens when a man is rude and mean towards you.

Example: you and your partner have a disagreement on something and he curses at you and calls you names that are disrespectful.

The way you handle his behavior is going to set the precedence for your relationship.

What you do is maintain your composure and calm your temper. Despite the fact that you may be so angry, do not go there with him. Do not lose your cool and start shouting because being angry won't help you, it will give him way to much power over your emotions.

Do this instead: ask him calmly if he thinks its okay for him to talk to you in that manner. Ask him if that is how he normally behaves and wait for his responds. If he is full of excuses, leave immediately and go home. Show him that you will not tolerate his actions and you are not afraid to lose him and that you won't want anyone to treat you with disrespect. Put your self-respect above your emotions. Walk away and see what he does. When he realizes what he has done he'll come asking for forgiveness.

He may call you the next day and act like nothing happened and that is not okay at all. If 'I'm sorry ' is not the first word he says then end the conversation and refuse to talk to him. If he still doesn't acknowledge his mistakes and doesn't apologize, then you are free to leave him to avoid getting into an abusive relationship.

7. Family test

This is where a guy takes you to his family. This where you need to talk about yourself because in this situation unlike the Bro Test, his family wants to get to know you. His family will probably ask you questions related to this:

    a. Your religion

    b. Your work

    c. What you like to do for fun

    d. Your family

You don't have to have everything figured out before you visit them but you should be able to say something about each of this part of your life. If you can't answer any of those questions then you have a big question.

8. The wife material test

Here the man decides if you are the woman he wants to spend the rest of his life with.

Do you both have the same goal? Do you have any plans for your future together? Do you like cooking? Is your house a disaster? Can you take care of and clean the house? Are you good with children?

Men are always careful about these things when choosing a woman to settle down with.

You have to be a woman for yourself. Don't lose your self-respect and self-respect to please a man, don't manipulate and don't try to be perfect

Conclusion

Understand that test do happen and know that as much as a man is testing you, you also need a high value man, so you should also be testing him too. Good luck!!

Printed in Great Britain
by Amazon